SHORT CIRCULAR WALKS IN THE AMBER VALLEY

by

JOHN N. MERRILL

Maps and photographs by John N. Merrill

TRAIL CREST PUBLICATIONS Ltd.,
- *"from footprint to finished book."*

1993

Sandia Mountains
New Mexico. USA

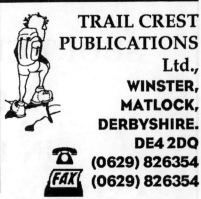

TRAIL CREST
PUBLICATIONS
Ltd.,
WINSTER,
MATLOCK,
DERBYSHIRE.
DE4 2DQ
☎ (0629) 826354
FAX (0629) 826354

Edited, typeset, designed, paged, printed, marketed and distributed by John
N. Merrill.

© Text & walks - John N. Merrill 1993
© Maps-John N. Merrill/Suncrest
Ventures Ltd., 1993.
© Photographs - John N. Merrill 1993.

First Published - August 1993

ISBN 1 874754 16 0

U.S.A.
office -
P.O.Box 124.
Santa Rosa,
New Mexico.
88435
U.S.A.

Please note - The maps in this guide are purely illustrative. You are
encouraged to use the appropriate 1:25,000 O.S. map.
Meticulous research has been undertaken to ensure that this publication is
highly accurate at the time of going to press. The publishers, however, cannot
be held responsible for alterations, errors or omissions, but they would welcome notification of such for future editions.

Typeset in - Bookman - bold, italic and plain 9pt and 18pt.

Printed by - John N. Merrill at Milne House, Speedwell
Mill, Miller's Green, Wirksworth, Derbyshire. DE4 4BL
Cover sketch - "The River Derwent, near Ambergate"
by John Creber. © Suncrest Ventures Ltd.

An all British
product.

ABOUT JOHN N. MERRILL

Born in the flatlands of Bedfordshire he soon moved to
Sheffield and discovered the joy of the countryside in the
Peak District, where he lives. A keen walker who travels
the world exploring mountains and trails. Over the last
twenty years he has walked more than 150,000 miles -
including the first walk around the entire coastline of
Britain, 7,000 miles - and worn out over sixty pairs of
boots. He has written more than 120 walk guides to areas
in Britain and abroad, and created numerous challenge
walks which have been used to raise more than £500,000
for charity. New Mexico, USA is his second home.

CONTENTS

INTRODUCTION

The Amber Valley is a fascinating area lying between the Matlocks. the Peak District and Derby. The northern area, now immortalised as "Peak Practice" Country, is rugged and hilly with stunning views of the Amber Valley. The southern is more gentle countryside with little used rights of way. These fourteen walks attempt to show the diversity of the area, some into well know places while other explore "forgotten" areas full of character and beauty.

The Lea Bridge and Crich walk take in many of the places associated with the hit T.V. series - *"Peak Practice."* to places like Lea, Dethick, Crich, Holloway, South Wingfield. The Alfreton walk will come as a surprise and is most scenic. The Whatstandwell, Heage, and Codnor based walks explore sections of the abandoned Cromford Canal but bring you to many historical features such as Codnor Castle and Heage windmill. Alport Height explores the high country of the area while the Whatstandwell, Belper and Duffield walks explore the Derwent Valley. All three interlink and can be done as one long walk or two medium length ones. The two western walks - Shottle and Weston Underwood - pass through quite peaceful countryside, not walked often but deserve exploring. While on the eastern side is the Horsley and Shipley Country Park walks. Again quieter and flatter countryside but two walks steeped in history.

These then are my favourite walks in the area. I hope you derive as much pleasure as I have from walking them over the years. May I wish you ....

Happy walking!
John N. Merrill

ABOUT THE WALKS

Whilst every care is taken detailing and describing the walk in this book, it should be borne in mind that the countryside changes by the seasons and the work of man. I have described the walk to the best of my ability, detailing what I have found on the walk in the way of stiles and signs. Obviously with the passage of time stiles become broken or replaced by a ladder stile or even a small gate. Signs too have a habit of being broken or pushed over. All the route follow rights of way and only on rare occasions will you have to overcome obstacles in its path, such as a barbed wire fence or electric fence. On rare occasions rights of way are rerouted and these ammendments are included in the next edition.

The seasons bring occasional problems whilst out walking which should also be borne in mind. In the height of summer paths become overgrown and you will have to fight your way through in a few places. In low lying areas the fields are often full of crops, and although the pathline goes straight across it may be more practical to walk round the field edge to get to the next stile or gate. In summer the ground is generally dry but in autumn and winter, especially because of our climate, the surface can be decidedly wet and slippery; sometimes even gluttonous mud!

These comments are part of countryside walking which help to make your walk more interesting or briefly frustrating. Standing in a farmyard up to your ankles in mud might not be funny at the time but upon reflection was one of the highlights of the walk!

The mileage for each walk is based on three calculations -

1. pedometer reading.
2. the route map measured on the map.
3. the time I took for the walk.

I believe the figure stated for each walk to be very accurate but we all walk differently and not always in a straight line! The time allowed for each walk is on the generous side and does not include pub stops etc. The figure is based on the fact that on average a person walks 2 1/2 miles an hours but less in hilly terrain.

Alport Stone -
Alport Height walk.

River Derwent, Belper - Belper walks.

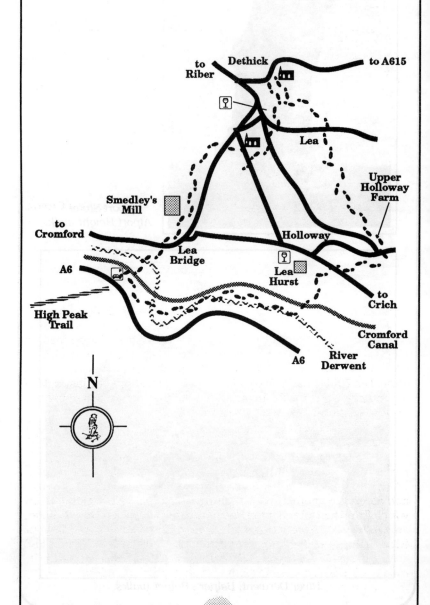

LEA
& DETHICK
- 5 MILES
- allow 2 hours

- Cromford Canal - Lea Bridge - Holloway - Lea - Dethick Church - Lea - Upper Holloway Farm - Holloway - Cromford Canal - Car park.

O.S. MAP *- 1:25,000 Pathfinder Series Sheet No. 794 (SK35) - Crich & Bullbridge.*

- Just off the Lea Bridge road close to the Cromford Canal. Grid Ref. SK315561.

- just off the route in Lea and Holloway.

ABOUT THE WALK - A very historical walk. Lea is famed for Florence Nightingale - *"the lady with the lamp"*. Dethick is famed for the Babington family; Anthony Babington being involved in the famous plot to release Mary Queen of Scots. Lea has the beautiful rhoderdendrons gardens to look at, just off the route - at their best in June. Lea Bridge has Smedley Mill and its mill shop. The last mile of the route is along the Cromford Canal. All together an absorbing two hour walk, with a pub nearly half-way!

WALKING INSTRUCTIONS - Return to the road and walk up it to the junction at Lea Bridge. Turn left, along Lea Road, past Smedley's mill and shop and past the mill pond on your left. Keep on the road for 1/2 mile to a footpath sign and walled path on your right. Turn right and ascend to another road. Turn right and pass Christ Church on your left and just after Repton House, turn left and ascend to woodland. Follow the path upwards to your left to a road and kissing gate. To your left are the Lea Rhoderdendron gardens. Cross over to a path and continue beside the playing fields to a road in Lea. Turn left along the road to a T junction. Cross to your right and cross the children's playing field to the main road. To your left is the inn! Turn right then left, as footpath signed - *"Dethick."* Descend and cross a stream and ascend through Swinepark Wood to a stile. Turn left to Dethick Church.

Return to the wood but continue along the righthand side of the field to another stile. Turn right and descend through woodland, cross a stream and ascend to the road. Turn right and in a few yards just after a chapel turn left on a lane past the houses to a footpath sign - *"Upper Holloway."* Gain a stile on your right and cross the fields diagonally to the top lefthand corner, where there is a stile. Continue to another and reach a sunken path. Turn right along it to a stile. Continue straight ahead, guided by stiles and walk beside a wall on your left to reach Upper Holloway Farm and road at a stile and footpath sign. Turn left then right to a footpath sign - *"Wakebridge"* , on your left. A few yards along the path turn right and descend steeply to the road in Holloway. Cross over and walk along the path/ lane which soon curves round to your right to a road. Turn left and in a few yards turn right, at the corner, for a stile on your right, with a house on its left. Walk past the house to a kissing gate. Continue on a track - to your right is Lea Hurst, the former home of Florence Nightingale. Descend to a kissing gate and the Cromford Canal. Turn right and follow the canal for a mile to the junction with the High Peak Trail, and turn right and cross the railway line and River Derwent back to the car park.

Path to Dethick church.

Lea Hurst - the former home of Florence Nightingale.

CRICH & WINGFIELD MANOR - 5 1/2 MILES

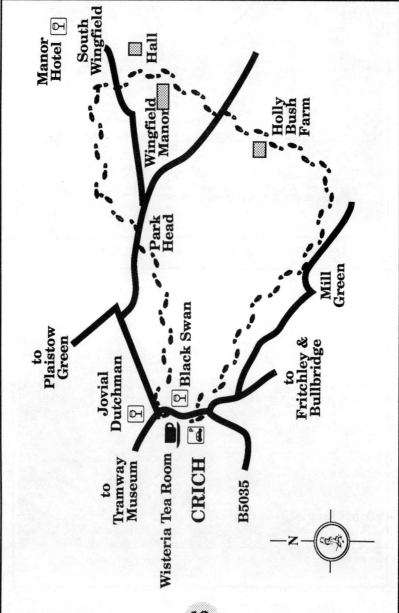

CRICH & WINGFIELD MANOR
- 5 1/2 MILES
- allow 2 hours.

- *Crich - Mill Green - Holly Bush Farm - Wingfield Manor - South Wingfield - Rough Farm - Park Head - Crich.*

 1:25,000 Pathfinder Series Sheet No. 794 (SK35) - Crich & Bullbridge.

- Central Crich.

- Jovial Dutchman & Black Swan, Crich. Manor Hotel in South Wingfield, just off the route.

- Wisteria Tea Room, central Crich.

ABOUT THE WALK - Outstanding! The section from Mill Green to Wingfield Manor is exceptionally attractive with views to Heage Windmill, the Amber Valley and the ruins of Wingfield Manor; certainly a walk to savour. Wingfield Manor, built by the Shrewsbury's, was one of the Derbyshire "goals" of Mary Queen of Scots in the 1580's. The ruins now cared for by English Heritage, was battered during the Civil War. Crich, South Wingfield and Wingfield Manor have all featured in the hit drama series on ITV - *"Peak Practice."*

WALKING INSTRUCTIONS - From the centre of Crich, infront of the Baptist Church dated 1877, cross the road to the narrow lane beside the wool shop. Pass the school and at the end of the houses and lane is a stile. Continue ahead on the right of woodland to a track. Cross to a stile and keep to the lefthand side of a mound - the path is undefined. In 120 yards cross to the otherside of the field boundary and walk beside it on your right. Continue onto another field, now keeping the field boundary on your left and gain a stile. At the end of the next field, another stile before the lane from Crich. Keep ahead and pass Ladybird Cottage in Mill Green. Just after is a drive. Walk up here a few yards to a stile on your right. Turn right and contour round two fields to a stone stile and woodland. Walk through to a stile and open country - ahead can been the base of an old windmill. Bear slightly left keeping the field boundary (a wall) on your right to the next stile and walled track. Turn right then left after a few yards, and descend the field to a stile. Here pick up a track and continue descending then ascending to Holly Bush Farm. Walk through the farm along the track to a lane - Park Lane. Crossover to a stile and continue onto a track, following it round to your left towards Manor Farm. At a stile keep right, and walk along the righthand side of the ruins of Wingfield Manor. Follow the track round to your left, past Wingfield Hall on your right, and onto the road - Manor Road - on the outskirts of South Wingfield.

Turn left and descend 100 yards to a stile on your right. Turn right and follow the path by the hedge to another stile. Partway through the next field turn left to a stile and stepping stones over Boggy Brook. Ascend the next three fields, keeping to the lefthand side, and using the stiles. In the fourth field the field boundary is on your right. Basically keep straight ahead across the fields, guided by stiles, passing Rough Farm on your left. Cross a track and gain the lane at Park Head. Cross to your right to a stile and keep the wall on your right. Continue beside the field boundary to a road leading to a tipping site on your left. Cross, as footpath signed and begin ascending two fields. Partway through the second field turn right to a stile and onto a lane - Roes Lane - on the outskirts of Crich, opposite Old Ends House. Turn left to the road junction beside the Jovial Dutchman Inn. Turn left and descend the road back into central Crich.

Central Crich.

CRICH - Crich Stand, built in 1923, stands on the site of previous towers, and is a permanent memorial to the Nottinghamshire and Derbyshire Regiments of the Sherwood Foresters. An annual pilgrimage is held on the first Sunday in July. On the northern side of the village is the National Tramway Museum, where trams from all over the world can be seen and travelled upon.

Wingfield Manor.

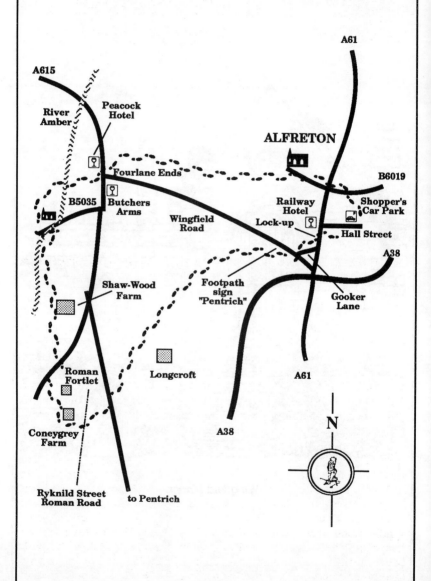

ALFRETON
AND
OAKERTHORPE
- 6 MILES
- Allow 2 1/2 hours.

- Alfreton - A615 - Longcroft - Coneygrey Farm - Shaw Wood - South Wingfield Church - Oakerthorpe - Alfreton.

 - 1:25,000 Pathfinder Series Sheets Nos.
- 795 (SK 45/55) - Sutton in Ashfield.
- 794 (SK35) - Crich & Bullbridge.

 - Central Alfreton - Shopper's car park.

Peacock Hotel & Butcher's Arms, Oakerthorpe. Several in Alfreton.

ABOUT THE WALK - Starting from Alfreton you pass the old Lockup, before crossing the fields to the Amber Valley. Here you have extensive views to Crich and Wingfield Manor. You walk through attractive woodland to the solitary church at South Wingfield - near the door is the tomb to George Hill who died 9.11.1835 aged 46, leaving a widow and ten children. Leaving the River Amber you ascend to Oakerthorpe and its inns before crossing the fields back to Alfreton. Most of the walk is well stiled and a clear path.

WALKING INSTRUCTIONS - Starting from the central car park in Alfreton, return to the road - Hall Street - and turn right along it to the A61, with Speeds on your right, and the Railway Hotel opposite. Turn left along the A61 - King Street, passing the Devonshire Arms and old lockup. Turn right along Gooker Lane to the A615 and turn right. 1/4 mile along here - Wingfield Road - at House No. 30 turn left, as footpath signed - *" Pentrich 2 miles. Oakerthorpe."* Follow the path between the houses to a stile and bear right beside the house gardens to another stile. Here angle left and cross the field to another stile and descend to woodland and a footbridge. Cross this and another one and turn left to a stile on the wood's edge. Cross the righthand corner of the field to a stile and turn left, keeping the field hedge on your left.

Continue to the fields end to a stile before a track. Cross over to another stile and cross the next field to its far righthand corner to a stile. In a few yards cross another stile and descend the field to gate gap before a minor road. Cross to a stile and walk across the field passing an electricity pole to a gate before a track. Turn right along the hedged track to Coneygrey Farm.

Walk through the farm and turn right along the track, along the "ridge" with the River Amber far below. Just before the farm you crossed the line of the Roman road - "Ryknild Street" and just past the farm you gain the site of a Roman fortlet. Go through a stile and descend the field to the far lefthand corner, where there is a stile. Turn right along the B6013 road for 100 yards to a stile on your left. Turn left and descend, cross a stream in woodland, and gain a stile. Continue across the field to the lefthand side of Shaw Wood Farm. Turn right along the tarmaced drive to a stile. Continue ahead along the lefthand side of the field to another stile and track through Shaw Wood; on your left is the main railway line. Follow the track for 1/2 mile to the B5035 road. Turn left and pass under the railway bridge and in 50 yards turn right at a stile past South Wingfield church to another stile, on its right. Continue ahead to another stile with the River Amber just to your left. A few yards later turn right and cross the railway bridge and continue straight ahead. In 1/4 mile gain the A615 road on the right of the Peacock Hotel at Oakerthorpe. Turn left then right and walk through Lamb Farm and guided by stiles keep to the lefthand side of the fields for the next 1/2 mile. Here you keep the field boundary on your right and soon gain a track. Keep on the track for more than 1/2 mile to the left of Alfreton church. Turn right and walk through the churchyard to the road and onto the crossroads in Alfreton. Either keep straight ahead to the shopping precinct with the car park behind, or turn right along the road to Speeds and left along Hall Street back to your start.

Old lock-up, Alfreton.

South Wingfield church.

Peacock Hotel, Oakerthorpe.

CROMFORD CANAL
& ALDERWASLEY - 6 MILES

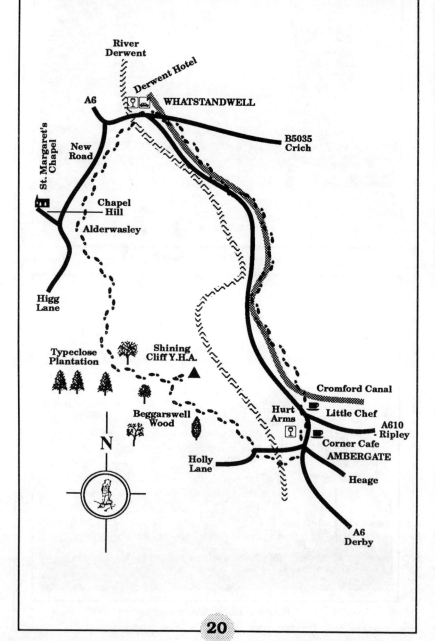

CROMFORD CANAL & ALDERWASLEY - 6 MILES
- allow 2 hours.

- - - - *- Whatstandwell - Cromford Canal - Ambergate - River Derwent - Beggarswell Wood - Shining Cliff YHA - Typeclose Plantation - Park Plantation - Alderwasley Park - Alderwasley - Whatstandwell.*

1:25,000 Pathfinder Series Sheet No. 794 (SK35) - Crich & Bullbridge.

- Small parking area beside canal at Whatstandwell.

- Derwent Hotel, Whatstandwell. Hurt Arms, Ambergate.

Corner Cafe and Little Chef, Ambergate.

ABOUT THE WALK - First you walk along a section of the abandoned Cromford Canal. Water fills the canal and bridges have rope grooves, made when the canal was in use over a century ago. From Ambergate you enter beautiful woodland to gain Shining Cliff YHA. From here you cross fields with magnificent views to Crich to reach the hamlet of Alderwasley. The old chapel dedicated to St. Margaret is worth seeing before walking down the lane back to Whatstandwell.

WALKING INSTRUCTIONS - At Whatstandwell gain the Cromford Canal towpath and turn right and walk beside the canal, on your left, for approximately 2 miles. After nearly a mile pass a bridge with rope groves, and nearly 2 miles the St John's Ambulance brigade adventure centre on your right. Upto to now the A6 road and railway line have not been far away from you on your right. Just after St. John's is a bridge. Continue beside the canal for another 1/4 mile, now curving left, to the next road bridge. Here leave the canal and turn right along Chase Road. Pass under the railway bridge and gain the A6 at Ambergate. Turn left past the Little Chef on your left, then Hurt Arms on your right and

Corner Cafe on your left. Continue on the A6 for another 100 yards to Holly Lane on your right. Turn right along the lane and over the River Derwent (cover sketch).

Just after where the lane turns left, turn right, as bridlepath signed, and walk along a track through woodland. Keep to the upper track, which becomes tarmaced as you pass several houses; the last one is called Glenside. You are now in Beggarswell Wood - part of the Crich Pioneers property. Where the path forks keep right and descend slightly to a small lake. Just before it turn right - signed YHA. You soon turn left and ascend to Shining Tor YHA. Turn left past the hostel and along the track, walking past gritstone outcrops and through Typeclose Plantation. In a 1/3 mile before a stile, turn right and ascend a track for a few yards to a gate and open fields. Go through the gate and keep the wall on your right to another gate and walk through Park Plantation. Just afterwards the now well defined track curves left and keeps to the lefthand side of Alderwasley Park. Ahead can be seen the white Georgian building of Alderwasley Hall, now a school. Reaching the road - Higg Lane - well to the left of it, turn right, past All Saints church to the road junction with Chapel Hill. Just up here on your right is St. Margaret's Chapel. Continue straight ahead on New Road for 3/4 mile towards the A6 road at Whatstandwell. Just before the road turn right, as footpath signed, and descend to the A6 close to the bridge. On the otherside is where you began.

CROMFORD CANAL - Completed in the late 18th century, running from Arkwright's Mill at Cromford to Langley Mill; here joining the Erewash and Nottingham canals. The section from Cromford to Ambergate is water filled and the rest to Langley Mill can still be traced - see my Canal Walks Vol. 1 - *"Short Circular walks on the Canals of Derbyshire & Nottinghamshire."*

ALDERWASLEY - St. Margaret's Chapel is mostly 16th century and is no longer used. All Saints church was built in 1850.

Cromford Canal, midway between Whatstandwell and Ambergate.

St. Margaret's Chapel, Alderwasley.

BELPER & AMBERGATE
- 6 1/2 MILES

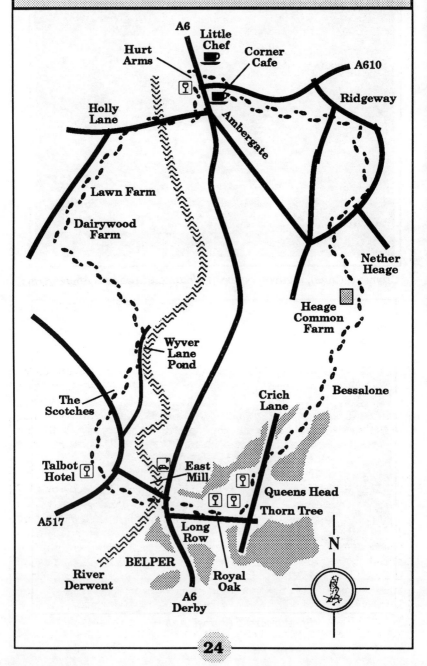

BELPER & AMBERGATE - 6 1/2 MILES

- allow 2 1/2 hours.

•• •• •• - *Belper - The Scotches - Wyver Lane - Coppice Wood - Dairywood Farm - Ambergate - Ridgeway - Nether Heage - Bessalone - Long Row - Belper.*

O.S. MAP - *1:25,000 Pathfinder Series Sheet Nos. -*
- 811 (SK 24/34) - Belper.
- 794 (SK35) - Crich & Bullbridge.

- *Riverside Gardens, near East Mill, Belper.*

(in walking order!) - Talbot Hotel, Belper. Hurt Arms, Ambergate. Queens Head, Thorn Tree, Royal Oak, Belper.

- *Corner Cafe and Little Chef, Ambergate.*

ABOUT THE WALK - Beautiful walking around the Derwent Valley between Ambergate and Belper. First you pass the Wyver Lane Pond (Derbyshire Wildlife Trust site complete with hide), before ascending with views north to Crich. You descend to Ambergate before ascending to Nether Heage and splendid views to Heage's six sail windmill. You cross fields before descending back into Belper via the historic Long Row. The route has several "refreshment points" along the way!

WALKING INSTRUCTIONS - From the car park return to the road and turn right and right again along Bridge Foot, passing East Mill on your right. Cross the River Derwent with views of the weirs and beyond to the gardens. Turn right along Belper Lane, with the Talbot Hotel on your left. Ascend the road to the first lefthand bend. Here keep straight ahead, as footpath signed, and walk along *The Scotches*. At the end of the road gain a stile and continue ahead along the field edge. Beyond keep a small wood on your right before descending gently to the lefthand side of another wood. Here is a stile and walk along the edge of the wood, descending to Wyver Lane. Turn left along the lane and on your right is Wyver Lane Pond. A little further along the lane is a hide.

Follow the lane for over 1/2 mile past the wall of a former rifle range on your left. Continue on a track with Coppice Wood on your left. Where the track turns right to Lawn Cottage, bear slightly left to a stile. Keep the edge of a wood on your left and where it turns left keep ahead and ascend the field to the lefthand corner of another wood. Here is a stile and continue ascending to another stile and lane. Turn right and follow this lane for 1/2 mile, past Dairywood Farm and Lawn Farm. At the road junction 1/4 mile later turn right - Holly Lane - and descend steeply to a bridge over the River Derwent and onto the A6 road at Ambergate. On your left is a cricket field.

Turn left along the A6 and opposite the Hurt Arms turn right along the Ripley Road. Walk along the road for 1/4 mile and just after passing under the railway bridge, turn right, as footpath signed, and follow the path/track past the Sewage Works. Walk through woodland (Thackers Wood) and past Thackers Villas on your right and onto the road junction at Ridgeway. Turn right, not sharp right, and walk along Ridgeway lane. In 100 yards and reaching your first houses on your right (Clovelly) turn right up a drive past a British Telecom building on your right. Beyond gain a stile and walk along the field edge beside the hedge on your right, for two fields to a stile. Turn left then right through another stile and follow the defined path across the field to Glenton Cottage and Gun Lane. Turn left along the lane into Nether Heage and in 100 yards turn right along Malthouse Lane. At the top turn right along Spanker Lane and turn left after 10 yards, as footpath signed, and walk along the track to Heage Common Farm.

Approaching the farm keep left to a stile and walk along the lefthand side of the fields, guided by stiles. In 1/4 mile go through another stile and turn right, with a stone wall on your left. At the next stile turn left and aim for the righthand side of a small wooded knoll - Bessalone. The path is well defined and very well stiled as you cross several fields to the outskirts of the houses on the fringe of Belper. Gaining the road turn left and in a few yards right on a tarmaced path. Keep on this for the next 1/2 mile inbetween the houses. Cross two roads before gaining Crich Lane. Bear left along it and pass the Queens Head Inn. Just after and before the Thorn Tree Inn turn right through the alley to Mill Street. Descend this to the bottom and the Royal Oak Inn. Turn right into Long Row and descend this to the A6 road. Turn right and you are back at East Mill, where you began.

Belper - East Mill archway with gun port on right.

Wyver Lane Pond.

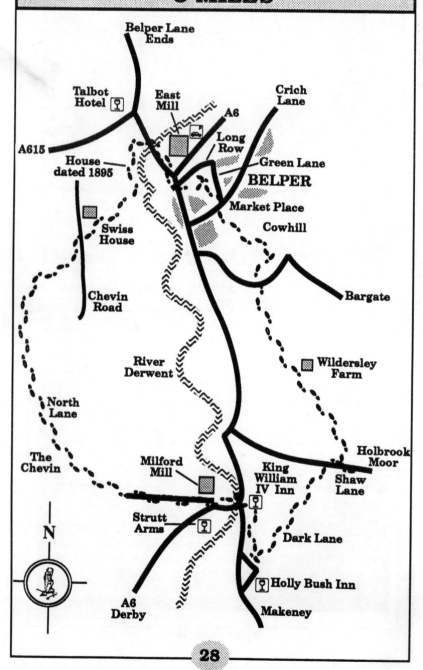

BELPER
AND
THE CHEVIN
- 6 MILES

- allow 2 1/2 hours.

•• •• •• - *Belper, East Mill - Chevinside - North Lane - The Chevin - Milford - Holbrook Moor - Wildersley Farm - Cowhill - Belper Market Place - Long Row - Belper, East Mill.*

 1:25,000 Pathfinder Series Sheet No. 811 (SK 24/34) - Belper.

 Beside Belper East Mill/Riverside Gardens.

In walking order - Talbot Hotel, Belper. Strutt Arms, King William IV, Milford. Holly Bush Inn, Makeney. Black Swan, Market Place, Royal Oak, near Long Row, Belper.

ABOUT THE WALK - One of my favourite walks in the area and one that I have often written about! After crossing the River Derwent you walk beside it a short distance before ascending to The Chevin with its absorbing views of the Derwent valley. You descend to Milford and the river and walk back along the eastern side of the valley, returning through Belper via the historic Long Row. As can be seen there are numerous inns along the way! The walk is done anti-clockwise.

Note - There are three walks in the Derwent valley in this book, between Ambergate and Duffield and can all be linked together for a 12 or 18 mile walk!

WALKING INSTRUCTIONS - From the car park beside East Mill return to the A6 road and turn right and right again, along Bridge Foot. Pass the mill and cross the bridge over the River Derwent, with the weirs on your right. At the end of the bridge turn left, as footpath signed, and follow the path, first beside the river on your left then away from it. It is well defined and in little over 1/4 mile reach a stile by a house on your left dated 1895. Continue ahead for 100 yards and bear right to a stile close to a spring. The path angles up to your left to the lefthand side of Swiss House. Turn right beside it to its drive and onto Chevin Road. Turn left and in 60 yards right at the stile and footpath sign, and ascend beside the field boundary for two fields to a track, close to Chevin Mount on your right. Turn left and follow this track - North Lane - for more than 1 1/4 miles, past a tower and trig point 125m. on your left, to a road. On your right is Chevin Golf Course. Descend the road past the former Royal Oak Inn, and onto a T junction. Cross and descend *"Chevin Alley"* to the A6 road, at Milford, with the Strutt Arms on your right.

Turn left past Milford Mill with its bell dated 1781, to the King William IV Inn. Turn right along the road to Makeney. Pass a garden centre on your right and in 1/4 mile turn left up Holly Bush Lane. At the top turn left, as footpath signed, along Dark Lane. To your right is the Holly Bush Inn. The lane is a track and in 1/4 mile pass Brownsgreen Farm. A further 1/4 gain Shaw Lane and turn right, towards Holbrook Moor. In about 100 yards turn left at a stile and footpath sign, close to the house, "The Homestead." The pathline keeps close to a wall on your right all the way to Wildersley Farm, nearly 1/2 mile away. Walk around the lefthandside of the farm and continue on a track past Rowlandhill Farm to the Holbrook Road. Turn right and where the road turns sharp right, on your left is a footpath sign and path. Turn left and follow the path around Cowhill - trig point 133m - with houses on your left. Reaching an open field descend "The Park", to Queen Street. Turn right to Belper Market Place. Follow the road past the Black Swan and turn left along Church Street. In a few yards turn left down Church Lane. At the bottom turn right along Green Lane, and follow it to its end. The second road on your left is Joseph Street, where the last Belper Nailer's workshop, can be seen. Continue to the end of the road and turn left down Long Row. At the bottom turn right and ahead is East Mill, where you began.

BELPER - Has an illustrious past with several centuries of nail making. In 1776 cotton spinning was started here by Sir Richard Arkwright and Jedediah Strutt. Long Row was originally built for the cotton workers.

MILFORD - Jedediah Strutt started a cotton spinning mill here in 1780. The stone bridge over the River Derwent dates from 1790. The River Derwent is Derbyshire's longest and mightiest river, being approximately 66 miles long.

River Derwent at Milford.

Long Row, Belper.

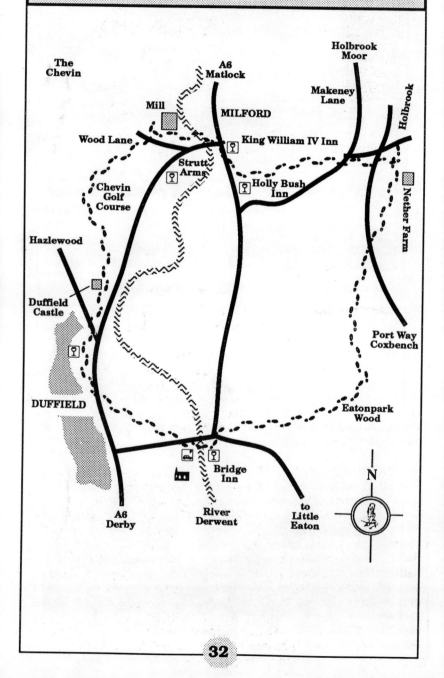

DUFFIELD
AND
MILFORD
- 6 MILES

- allow 2 1/2 hours.

Duffield Church - Bridge Inn - Eatonpark Wood - Daypark - Nether Farm - Holbrook - Makeney - Milford - Wood Lane - Courthouse Farm - Chevin Golf Course - Duffield Castle - Duffield - Duffield Church.

 1:25,000 Pathfinder Series Sheet No. 811 (SK 24/34) - Belper.

 - Near Duffield Church. Grid Ref. SK349428.

- in walking order - Bridge Inn, Duffield. Spotted Cow, Holbrook. Hollybush Inn, Makeney. King William IV Inn, Strutt Arms, Milford. Kings Head, White Hart Inn, Belper.

ABOUT THE WALK - A particularly attractive walk to the north of Derby. First you cross the fields to the River Derwent, before ascending high above the valley, following good paths to Holbrook. Here you gradually descend to Makeney and the river before ascending again to curve round the Chevin Golf Course back to Duffield. You walk through the village past the site of Duffield castle back to Duffield church. The walk is done anti-clockwise.

WALKING INSTRUCTIONS - Starting from Duffield church, go through the stile on the left of it and follow the path across the field to the River Derwent. Follow the path round to your left to the road bridge and cross it and turn right past the Bridge Inn. 100 yards later turn left along Eaton Bank. At the end turn right and soon ascend steps. Gain a gate and keep along the edge of the fields to stiles and gates. In more than 1/2 mile reach a stile and enter Eatonpark Wood. In 30 yards the path curves right, here turn left to a stile and footpath sign. Go straight across the field, heading northwards to a stile. Continue along the edge of the field to two more stiles and woodland on your left at Daypark. From here you bear right slightly to cross the field to a stile and footpath sign, close to a house. Turn left along the tarmaced lane and in 60 yards the lane curves right, here turn left at a stile and descend to a stream and footbridge in woodland. Cross to a stile and bear right across the field to another stile and road - Port Way. Turn right then left, as footpath signed, and follow the tarmaced lane past Nether Farm, 1/4 mile away. Shortly afterwards turn left down a walled path - to your right is Stony Lane - and enter Holbrook.

Turn left past the Spotted Cow and turn right along Mellor Lane. At the end turn left then right at the stile and footpath sign. Keep the fence on your left to a stile and continue ahead descending to another stile and on down to Holly Bush Lane at Makeney. On your left is the Holly Bush Inn. Turn right and descend to the road and turn right along it towards Milford and King William IV Inn. Reaching the A6 turn left over the road bridge over the River Derwent. Pass Milford Mill and before the Strutt Arms on your left, ascend *"Chevin Alley."* Cross the road at the top and continue ascending. About half-way up the hill turn left along Wood Lane. The track leads through woodland and onto Courthouse Farm, which you walk past on your left. Just afterwards turn left at a stile and descend to your left. Then bear right walking around the righthand side of Chevin Golf Course, on a well defined path. Reach the road near the club house and soon afterwards gain the A6 road. Turn right and in 30 yards on your right are the steps leading to the site and remains of Duffield Castle - National Trust property. Continue through Duffield for 1/2 mile past the Kings Head, White Hart Inn. Just after The Meadow house, turn left at a stile and walk diagonally across the field to a road bridge. Pass under it and soon afterwards turn left over a footbridge over the railway line and gain Duffield church and car park where you began.

Bridge Inn and River Derwent, Duffield.

Duffield church.

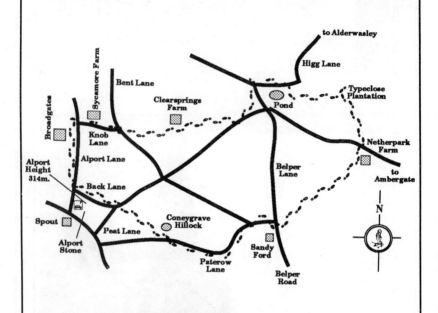

Alport Stone.

From opposite page -
and continue to two more to the lane at Ranch House. Turn right, leaving the lane, and walk along the track past Clearsprings Farm to a private house, Coldaston, reached via a stile. At the start of the drive is a stile and through this keep to the lefthand side of the field as you ascend to a lane. Turn right and where the lane forks keep left - Knob Lane - past Sycamore Farm to a T junction. Here turn left past Broadgates and ascend Alport Lane. In 1/4 mile you are back in familiar country as you approach Alport Height.

ALPORT HEIGHT
- 4 1/2 MILES

- allow 2 hours.

•• •• •• *- Alport Height - Coneygrave Hillock - Sandy Ford -
Netherpark Farm - Typeclose Plantation - Clearsprings Farm -
Sycamore Farm - Broadgates - Alport Height.*

 *- 1:25,000 Pathfinder Series Sheet No. 794 (SK35) - Crich
& Bullbridge.*

 - Alport Height.

 - None! Nearest at Ambergate or Wirksworth.

ABOUT THE WALK - Standing at 314m. (1,034 ft.) Alport Height is
the highest point in the Amber Valley district, and since 1930 has been
National Trust property. Just below the summit is a tall gritstone
Alport Stone. The view from the summit is extensive and on a clear day
five counties can be seen. The walk is a mixture of paths and quiet lanes
in this *"high"* country of the Amber Valley.

WALKING INSTRUCTIONS - From the car park return to the lane
and turn right. At the crossroads a few yards later, turn right along
Back Lane. (Alport Lane in front is your return route.) Walk along the
lane for over 1/4 mile to a T junction, with Peat Lane to your right.
Cross to a stile and go straight across the field to another. Continue
with a wall on your left to another and keep ahead to further stiles and
lane at Coneygrave Hillock. Turn left along the lane - Palerow Lane - to
a T junction, with Belper Road, 1/2 mile away. Turn right and in a few
yards left at a stile and footpath sign before Sandy Ford. Keep the wall
on your right to a gate and keep ahead to another gate; the wall curves
to your left. Continue on to a stile and gate at Netherpark Farm.
Basically go straight across the lane here, as guided by footpath signs
- YHA 1/2 mile, (Shining Tor.) The path which is a good track is now in
woodland and in just over 1/4 mile turn left at a stile. Continue on a
track through the trees and in less than 1/2 mile approach the end of
the wood with a pond to your left, and reach Higg Lane. Turn left and
in 120 yards at a road junction turn left. In 80 yards turn right at a stile
and footpath sign. The path goes diagonally left across the field to a stile

37

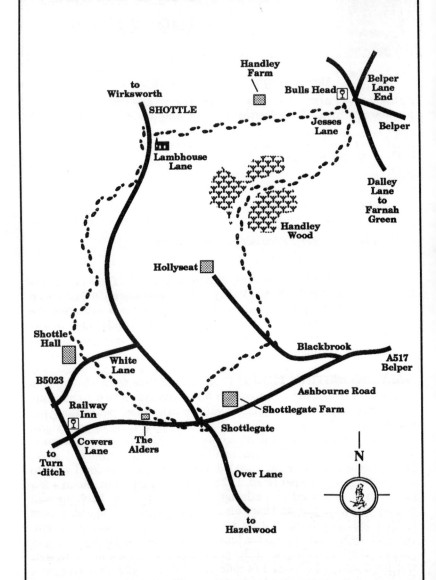

SHOTTLE &
BELPER LANE END
- 6 1/2 MILES
- allow 2 1/2 hours.

Shottle - Shottle Hall - Shottlegate - Handley Wood - Belper Lane End - Handley Farm - Shottle.

1:25,000 Pathfinder Series Sheet No. 811 (SK 24/34) - Belper.

- Limited roadside parking at Shottle and Belper lane Ends.

- Bull's Head, Belper Lane Ends.

ABOUT THE WALK - A walk in quiet countryside along little used rights of way. All the stiles and signs are there. The section through Handley Wood back to Shottle is exceptionally attractive, and surprisingly hilly! There is just one inn at Belper lane End, two thirds of the way round, and before the last "hill"! There is little parking along the route which I have started from Shottle - Grid Ref. SK 313495. The walk is done anti- clockwise.

WALKING INSTRUCTIONS - From Shottle walk down the lane - Lambhouse Lane - past Shottle church - your return path comes in here. About 120 yards from the church, where the lane curves left is a stile and path sign on your right. Turn right and basically keep to the righthand side of the fields, for 1/2 mile, as you curve round back to the lane - the whole section is well stiled. Regaining the lane turn right and in a few yards right again at a stile and path sign. The path line goes down to the barns on the righthand side of Shottle Hall, but if the field is full of crops you may be better to walk around the righthand side of the field. Walk along the lefthand side of the hall to White Lane. Cross over to a stile and path sign and keep the hedge on your right and where it turns right, angle slightly left across the field to the lefthand side of a house - *"The Alders"*, where there is a stile and path sign.

Turn left and ascend the road - Ashbourne Road - to the crossroads at Shottlegate, passing Hill Top Farm on your left. Turn left and pass the village hall - Shottlegate W.I. and just afterwards right, at a stile and footpath sign. Descend the field to the bottom where there is a stile. Continue to another soon afterwards with a footbridge. Continue slightly to your right to more stiles before descending to a footbridge over Shipley Brook, near Chapel House Farm (Blackbrook). Beyond reach a farm road via a stile. Turn left and in less than 1/4 mile turn right at a gate and follow a faint grass track across the field to a stile, just after crossing Black Brook. Continue ascending gently on the track to a stile on the edge of Handley Wood. Continue through the wood to a path junction in 200 yards. Here turn right and ascend on a good path through the trees to a stile on the wood's edge. Keep a wall on your right to a stile and on to another. Turn right then left past a small pond and continue with a wall on your right to an old lane. Cross over to a stile and path sign and bear diagonally left across the field to a stile. Here you have a choice - depending on the season. Either continue descending diagonally across the field towards Belper Lane End or descend directly down to the lane - Dalley Lane - and turn left to Belper Lane End; both are rights of way.

At the cross roads in Belper Lane End is the Bulls Head Inn. Just before it on your left is Jesses Lane. Turn left and ascend the lane which soon ends, but keep straight ahead along the edge of the field to a stile and small wood. Cross slightly to your left to a stile and old lane, you crossed earlier. A gate and footpath sign are opposite. Go through the gate and keep the wall on your right to the next field where you turn left and descend steeply to Hillside. Ahead can be seen a field boundary running westwards and that is your pathline back to Shottle. At the house turn left then right via the stiles and descending the field edge to *"stepping stones"* over Wilder Brook. Ascend the other side keeping close to the field edge, passing Handley Farm to your right. You now basically keep the field boundary on your right and you will come to all the stiles and reach Shottle little over 1/2 mile away - to the right of the church. Beautiful quiet crossing where only the skylark and curlew break the silence.

The Bulls Head, Belper Lane End.

REMEMBER AND OBSERVE THE COUNTRY CODE

Enjoy the countryside and respect its life and work.

 Guard against all risk of fire.

 Fasten all gates.

 Keep your dogs under close control.

Keep to public paths across farmland.

 Use gates and stiles to cross fences, hedges and walls.

 Leave livestock, crops and machinery alone.

 Take your litter home - pack it in; pack it out.

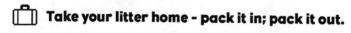 Help to keep all water clean.

 Protect wildlife, plants and trees.

 Take special care on country roads

Make no unnecessary noise.

41

HEAGE AND PENTRICH
- 7 MILES

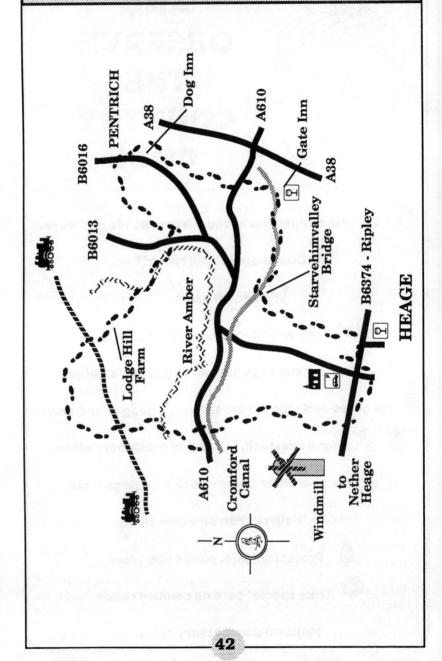

HEAGE
AND
PENTRICH
- 7 MILES
- allow 2 1/2 hours.

- *Heage - Windmill - Bullbridge - Sawmills - Wingfield Park Farm - Lodge Hill Farm - Wingfield Park - River Amber - Pentrich - Fields Farm - Cromford Canal - Starvehimvalley Bridge - Heage.*

 - 1:25,000 Pathfinder Series Sheet No. 794 (SK35) - Crich & Bullbridge.

- No official one. Roadside parking only.

Heage Tavern, White Hart Inn, Heage; Dog Inn, Pentrich; Gate Inn, Lower Hartshay.

ABOUT THE WALK - A delightful walk in the Amber Valley. First you cross the fields near the impressive six sailed Heage windmill *(Old Ned)*. As you descend from here you extensive views of the valley, before crossing the line of the Cromford Canal. You ascend and loop round across Wingfield Park and beside the River Amber before ascending to Pentrich. From here you gain a waterfilled section of the Cromford Canal and an impressive bridge (and name) - Starvehimvalley - before ascending back to Heage. I have started the walk from St. Luke's church in Heage, where there is roadside parking.

WALKING INSTRUCTIONS - Return to the main road - B6374 - in Heage, by the White Hart Inn. Turn right and right again along School Lane. Walk along the lane towards the end of the houses, for nearly 1/4 mile, to a footpath sign and stile on your right - *"Sawmills. Ladygrove."* In a few yards reach a stile on your right and continue along the field edge to another. Here turn left and aim for the top lefthand corner of the field where there is a stile. On your left is Heage windmill. You are now on the edge of the Amber Valley and the views from here as you descend are stunning. Descend to a stile and keep the hedge on your left to another. Continue descending bearing slightly left to seven more stiles to a gate and stile by a wall, in the valley bottom. Here turn right and soon walk along a walled path and onto a former bridge over the Cromford Canal, near thr Lockwood Group. Descend steps to the A610 road at Ladygrove/Sawmills, and turn left. In a few yards turn right at a stile with the Amber Playing Field on your right. Walk across the field to a footbridge over the River Amber.

Continue ahead to the railway line, which cross, and continue with the hedge on your right for a 1/3 mile to a stile and lane. Turn right along the lane for just over 1/4 mile, past the drive to Beech Hill Farm. Just after turn right at a stile and footpath sign - *"Wingfield Park."* Cross the field to another stile and track to Lodge Hill Farm. Walk past the farm on your right and descend slightly on the track to the perimeter wall of Wingfield Park. Here leave the track and descend to the River Amber and walk beside it to a footbridge. Cross and ascend to the road - B6013. Turn right and in a few yards is Hamlyn Mill dated 1878. Opposite is the stile and path sign - *"Pentrich 1 mile."* The path keeps straight ahead beside a field boundary before bearing left to a stile. Continue with the hedge on your right to another stile. Continue to gate and bear right. Ahead can be seen Pentrich church, your destination. Pass under an electricity line and onto a stile. Continue to the righthand side of the church, dedicated to St. Matthew. Near the main door is a gravestone to Ann Stirland who died on December 6th 1797, aged 97.

Reaching the road in Pentrich turn right and soon pass the Dog Inn on your left. Continue through the village for 1/4 mile to a No Through Road on your left. This soon becomes a track as you pass Fields Farm. Keep on this walled path to its end, ignoring the track to your right. Bear left at the end to a stile and the A610 road. Cross to your right to a tarmaced path and follow this to a minor road. Turn left and in a few yards before the Gate Inn, turn right and descend to the Cromford Canal. Keep the canal on your left and in 1/4 mile, approaching a row of houses, your can see the remains of a narrow boat. Cross the road and continue straight ahead past the houses on your right to a stile. The path is defined as walk along the line of the canal to a waterfilled area of it at Starvehimvalley Bridge. Cross the bridge to a stile and leave the canal. Bear right to a hedge and bear left and begin ascending the valley. You soon gain a track which you follow all the way back into Heage; the track becoming Bond Lane. Gaining the road - B6374 - opposite the Heage Tavern turn right to the White Hart Inn. Turn right back to St. Luke.

PENTRICH - Is famous for the Pentrich Rebellion of 1817. The three ringleaders, Jeremiah Brandreth, William Turner, and Isaac Ludlam where hung and drawn on November 8th in Derby. Their bodies were buried in a communal grave at St. Werburgh's church in Derby. Pentrich church, dedicated to St. Matthew, dates from Norman times.

HEAGE WINDMILL - *One of the best preserved examples of a tower mill, and is unusual having six sails.*

Starvehimvalley Bridge, Cromford Canal.

WESTON UNDERWOOD & MUGGINTON - 6 1/2 MILES

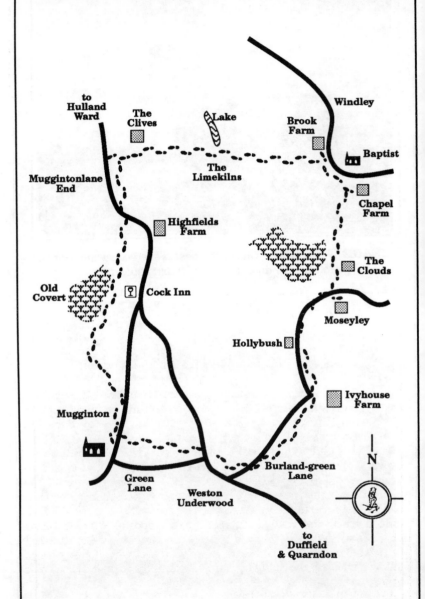

to Hulland Ward

The Clives

Lake

Windley

Brook Farm

Baptist

Muggintonlane End

The Limekilns

Chapel Farm

Highfields Farm

The Clouds

Old Covert

Cock Inn

Moseyley

Hollybush

Ivyhouse Farm

Mugginton

Green Lane

Weston Underwood

Burland-green Lane

N

to Duffield & Quarndon

WESTON UNDERWOOD & MUGGINTON - 6 1/2 MILES

- allow 2 1/2 hours.

▄▄ ▄▄ ▄▄ - *Weston Underwood - Burland-green Lane - Moseyley - Chapel Farm - Brook Farm - The Clives - Muggintonlane End - Old Covert - Mugginton - Weston Underwood.*

1:25,000 Pathfinder Series Sheet No. 811 (SK 24/34) - Belper.

None. Roadside parking in Weston Underwood.

- just off the route - Cock Inn, Mugginton; approx 3/4 of the way round the walk.

ABOUT THE WALK - A delightful quiet walk off the beaten track with an inn near the end. Mugginton church is full of interest and well worth exploring. The rights of way are little used but all the stiles and signs are there. The walk is done in an anti-clockwise direction.

WALKING INSTRUCTIONS - From Weston Underwood, walk to the eastern end of the village to a cross roads and turn left along Burland-green Lane. Follow the lane for 1 1/4 miles. Pass Ivyhouse Farm, and the solitary house Hollybush. Follow the lane round to your right past a wood on your left to Moseyley Farm on your right. Turn left through a gate and follow the farm track for a few yards before leaving it and keeping to the lefthand side of The Clouds. Slowly descend the field beyond aiming for the bottom lefthand corner, where there is a stile and footbridge. Keep to the righthand side of the fields to more stiles and onto a track and road at Chapel Farm, opposite Windley Baptist chapel. Turn left along the road - B5024 - and in 100 yards it turns right at Brook Farm. Here turn leave the road via a gate on your left and follow a track on the left of the farm. Beyond the farm leave the track and aim slightly to your right to a footbridge. Cross over and turn right and basically walk close to the brook. First it is on your right and after crossing another footbridge two fields later it is on your left. After three more stiles reach a gate and lake. Turn left then left again and ascend the field to a stile. Cross the next field to another stile, straight ahead. Continue close to the field boundary to more stiles and the track at The Clives. Beyond the building bear left at a stile and reach the road near Muggintonlane End.

Turn left along the road for just over 1/4 mile, past the houses. The road bears left and round the corner is a stile and footpath sign on your right. Walk around the field to the edge of woodland - Old Covert - where there is a stile. Keep to the edge of the field with woodland on your right to another stile. A path from here leads to the Cock Inn on your left. Continue beside the wood to another stile and just after leaving the wood is another stile at the end of the field. Continue across the fields guided by stiles and reach Mugginton in just over 1/4 mile. Turn right through the village and just before the church is a path sign and walled path. Turn left and follow this to a large field which you cross to a footbridge over Greenland Brook. Approaching the houses of Weston Underwood bear right to a gate and path sign. Turn left along Green Lane back into Weston Underwood. If visiting Mugginton church you can turn left afterwards and follow Green Lane back to Weston Underwood.

MUGGINTON CHURCH - Dedicated to All Saints the building dates from the 12th century and is notable for its gargoyle carvings, the story of the Green man, oak ceiling and 1,400 year old yew tree.

EQUIPMENT NOTES
... some personal thoughts

BOOTS - *preferably with a full leather upper, of medium weight, with a vibram sole. I always add a foam cushioned insole to help cushion the base of my feet.*

SOCKS - *I generally wear two thick pairs as this helps minimise blisters. The inner pair are of loop stitch variety and approximately 80% wool. The outer are a thick rib pair of approximately 80% wool.*

WATERPROOFS - *for general walking I wear a T shirt or cotton shirt with a cotton wind jacket on top. You generate heat as you walk and I prefer to layer my clothes to avoid getting too hot. Depending on the season will dictate how many layers you wear. In soft rain I just use my wind jacket for I know it quickly dries out. In heavy or consistant rain I slip on a neoprene lined cagoule, and although hot and clammy it does keep me reasonably dry. Only in extreme conditions will I don overtrousers, much preferring to get wet and feel comfortable. I never wear gaiters!*

FOOD - *as I walk I carry bars of chocolate, for they provide instant energy and are light to carry. In winter a flask of hot coffee is welcome. I never carry water and find no hardship from not doing so, but this is a personal matter! From experience I find the more I drink the more I want and sweat. You should always carry some extra food such as trail mix & candy bars etc., for emergencies.*

RUCKSACKS - *for day walking I use a climbing rucksack of about 40 litre capacity and although it leaves excess space it does mean that the sac is well padded, with an internal frame and padded shoulder straps. Inside apart from the basics for one day I carry gloves, balaclava, spare pullover and a pair of socks.*

MAP & COMPASS - *when I am walking I always have the relevant map - preferably 1:25,000 scale - open in my hand. This enables me to constantly check that I am walking the right way. In case of bad weather I carry a compass, which once mastered gives you complete confidence in thick cloud or mist.*

CODNOR, CASTLE & COMFORD CANAL - 6 MILES

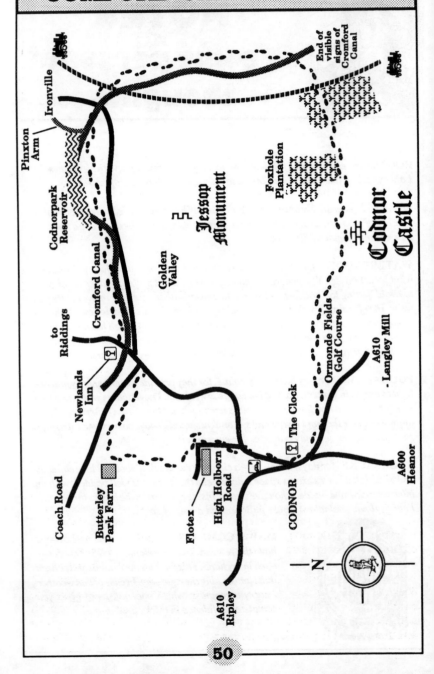

Coach Road

Butterley Park Farm

Newlands Inn

to Riddings

Cromford Canal

Flotex

High Holborn Road

Codnorpark Reservoir

Pinxton Arm

Ironville

Golden Valley

Jessop Monument

Foxhole Plantation

End of visible signs of Cromford Canal

Codnor Castle

Ormonde Fields Golf Course

The Clock

CODNOR

A610 - Langley Mill

A600 Heanor

A610 Ripley

N

CODNOR, CASTLE & CROMFORD CANAL - 6 MILES

- allow 2 1/2 hours.

⬛ ⬛ ⬛ *Codnor - Butterley Park Farm - Golden Valley - Cromford Canal - Codnor Park - Foxhole Plantation - Codnor Castle - Ormonde Fields - Codnor.*

O.S. MAP - *1:25,000 Pathfinder Series Sheet Nos.*
- *812 (SK 44/54) - Nottingham (North) and Ilkeston.*
- *No. 795 (SK 45/55) - Sutton in Ashfield.*

🚗P - *Central Codnor. Two small ones beside Codnorpark Reservoir.*

🍷 - *The Clock, Codnor. Newlands Inn, Golden Valley.*

ABOUT THE WALK - Outstanding! Full of interest and through very pleasant countryside. You follow a major section of the abandoned Cromford Canal and see where the Pinxton arm started at Ironville. You ascend to the fascinating ruins of Codnor Castle before regaining Codnor. The walk is done clockwise and follows good paths.

WALKING INSTRUCTIONS - From the car park in Codnor return to the lower road to Riddings. Walk along it past a house dated 1708 I ♥ W on it, before descending. Take the first road on your left - High Holborn Road. Part way up the road on your right is a stile. Follow the path here continuing upwards and turn left along it past the Flotex factory. Approaching some white cylinders turn right to a stile. Now in rural countryside, keep the hedge on your right and descend the field to a stile. Turn left and gain a track and follow this to the righthand side of Butterley Park Farm. Here reach Coach Road and turn right and descend the lane to the Riddings Road. Turn left and in a few yards, before the Newlands Inn, turn right - footpath signed - "Pinxton 3 1/4 miles." and gain the Cromford Canal on your right. Walk beside the canal and in a 1/3 mile cross a footbridge and continue on a wide path with Codnorpark Reservoir on your left. In another 1/3 mile cross a another footbridge and keep the canal on your right once more. In a few yards on your left is the canal bridge over the start of the Pinxton Arm of the canal. Keep beside the canal for the next mile, passing the remains of several locks. Close to end of the visible part of the canal are the remains of a railway bridge pillars.

Just after turn right and take the second path on your right and cross woodland to a footbridge over the railway line. Bear slightly to your right through woodland to a path sign. Here keep to the edge of the field to a stile on the edge of Foxhole Plantation. Keep along the edge to another stile and begin ascending. Ahead can be see the ruins of Codnor Castle. Aim for the righthand side of it to reach a stile and farm road at Castle Farm. Turn right to a stile. Keep the fence on your right to another stile. Here bear left across the Ormonde Fields Golf Course, aiming for the lefthand edge of a small wood around a house - Ormonde Fields. Gain a stile and cross the drive and walk around the lefthand side of the wood as you descend to a green. On the otherside in trees is a stile. Cross the edge of the field to another stile and turn left along the tarmaced drive. You can follow this back to Codnor or part way along the drive turn right at a stile and cross the playing field to Codnor.

CODNOR CASTLE - The present remains date from Henry 111 time and was built by the Grey family. An earlier castle stood here built by William Peveril in Norman times. The Grey's castle was extensive with courtyards, a moat and four towers. Much of the castle's stone has been used in many of the surround farms. The estate once covered 2,000 acres and the Jessop Monument can be seen clearly from Codnorpark Reservoir.

Canal bridge at the start of the Pinxton Arm of the Cromford Canal.

Ruins of Codnor Castle.

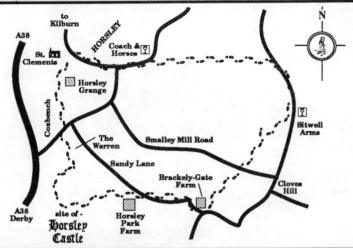

Sitwell Arms.

from opposite page - 1/4 mile to a track and footpath sign on your left. Turn left along the track and soon pass Horsley Gate Farm on your left. Follow the track round to woodland. Here there is a path on your left that goes around the site of Horsley Castle, woodland and gritstone outcrops. This path rejoins the track, 1/4 mile later, but is more interesting than the track. The track/path turns sharp right and descends to the wood's edge, with a fence on your left. At the stile turn right and ascend a short distance to a 3 way footpath sign. Turn left and descend by a wall to a footbridge, before the road at Coxbench. Turn right then left, as footpath signed and ascend over the hill, guided by stiles. Ahead can be seen Horsley church and aim for the right of it, coming to it on a walled path. Turn right back into Horsley and Church Street.

HORSLEY
- 5 MILES
- allow 2 hours.

 - *Horsley - Gypsy Brook - Hilltop Farm - Sitwell Arms - Marks Hill - Brackely Gate Farm - Horsley Park Farm - The Warren - Coxbench - Horsley.*

 1:25,000 Pathfinder Series Sheet No. 811 (SK 24/34) - Belper.

🚗 *- None. Roadside parking in Horsley.*

🍷 *Coach & Horses, Horsley. Sitwell Arms, near Smalley.*

ABOUT THE WALK - Horsley is an attractive village full of interest. This walk encircles the area and passes through very picturesque scenery. The wood and gritstone outcrops before Coxbench are most attractive and quite a surprise in this part of county. I enjoyed this walk very much.

WALKING INSTRUCTIONS - Starting from the near Horsley church, dedicated to St. Clements, walk up Church Street. Pass a fountain and Pillar Box dated 1869 on your right. Pass the Coach & Horses Inn on your left; just before it on your right is one pillar of Horsley stocks. Just afterwards between houses No. 6 & 8 is the footpath. Turn right here and pass between the houses to a stile. Bear left to another and aim for the righthand corner of the field to another. Keep the field hedge on your right to reach more stiles and in 1/4 mile gain a footbridge over Gypsy Brook. Continue to more stiles and a footbridge before reaching the road to Horsley Woodhouse in just over 1/4 mile. Here turn right along the road and in less than 1/4 mile, just before the Sitwell Arms, turn right at a stile and path sign. Keep the field boundary on your left to two stiles and a footbridge. Bear right slightly and continue along the field edge before bearing right to footbridges before reaching Smalley Mill Road. Go straight across to a stile and footpath sign - *"Cloves Hill."* Keep the hedge on your right and walk past a small plantation on your right to a stile. Bear slightly right to a wall, which you keep on your right as you walk just below Marks Hill and ascend to the road, where there is a stile and footpath sign, to the lefthand side of Brackely-Gate Farm.

Turn right along the lane - Sandy Lane - and keep on it for more than

SHIPLEY COUNTRY PARK - 5 MILES

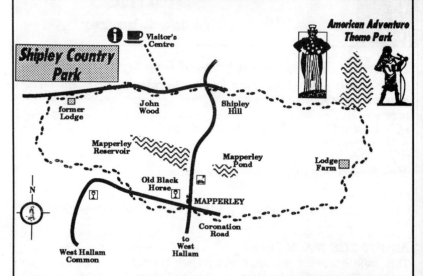

Mapperley.

from opposite page - around the edge for the former hall and bear right past Nottingham Lodge. The track/path now descends and becomes a great contrast from the peace and solitude as ahead is the American Adventure theme park! Descend around the perimeter fence and cross the end of Shipley Lake. Immediately turn right on the road and follow it round to Lodge Farm. Here keep left on the track, following round to a cross roads of paths. Turn right, still on a track. This leads into Coronation Road and Mapperley. Part way along here you can turn right, as footpath signed, to return to Mapperley Reservoir and car park.

SHIPLEY COUNTRY PARK
- 5 MILES
- allow 2 hours.

 - Mapperley - Mapperley Park - Whitehouse Farm - Shipley Park - Shipley Hill - American Adventure - Lodge Farm - Mapperley.

 1:25,000 Pathfinder Series Sheet No. 812 (SK 44/54) - Nottingham (North) and Ilkeston.

Mapperley lane end. Grid Ref. 435434.

Old Black Horse, Mapperley.

- Rambler's Coffee Shop - Visitor's Centre, 1/2 mile from route.

ABOUT THE WALK - Well defined paths and tracks around Shipley Country Park. The park, developed by the Derbyshire County Council and officially open on 26th May 1976, covers 600 acres and was part of the Miller Mundy estate in the 18th and 19th centuries. 1/2 mile off the route and well signed is the Visitor's centre and Ramblers Coffee Shop. The park is open from 9.00a.m. to dusk. The walk is done clockwise.

WALKING INSTRUCTIONS - Return to Mapperley village and turn right along the road past the Old Black Horse Inn. Follow the road for over 1/4 mile past the houses to a stile and footpath sign on your right. Cross to the lefthand corner of the field to a stile and bear left along a fence to a stile. Continue to another and enter woodland. The path is defined as you walk through to another stile. You now basically keep the field boundary - hedge - on your left for 1/2 mile to gain the stiles. After the third stile you bear right with the hedge on your right to a stile and lane - former estate road. Turn right and keep on this lane/track for the next 1 1/2 miles. Soon pass a former lodge and nearly a mile later a path to your right to Mapperley Reservoir. Nearly 1/4 mile later is a signed path on your left to the Visitor's Centre. Continue on the road to a road junction near Shipley Hill. Cross over to a track and walk

WALK RECORD CHART

Date walked -

LEA & DETHICK - 5 MILES ....

CRICH & WINGFIELD MANOR - 5 1/2 MILES ....

ALFRETON & OAKERTHORPE - 6 MILES ....

CROMFORD CANAL & ALDERWASLEY - 6 MILES ....

BELPER & AMBERGATE - 6 1/2 MILES ....

BELPER & THE CHEVIN - 6 MILES ....

DUFFIELD AND MILFORD - 6 MILES ....

ALPORT HEIGHT - 4 1/2 MILES ....

SHOTTLE & BELPER LANE END - 6 1/2 MILES ....

HEAGE AND PENTRICH - 7 MILES ....

WESTON UNDERWOOD & MUGGINTON - 6 1/2 MILES ....

CODNOR, CASTLE & CROMFORD CANAL - 6 MILES ....

HORSLEY - 5 MILES ....

SHIPLEY COUNTRY PARK - 5 MILES ....

JOHN MERRILL WALK BADGE

THE JOHN MERRILL WALK BADGE

Complete six of the walks in this guide and get the above special John Merrill walk badge and signed certificate. Badges are black cloth with figure and lettering embroidered in four colours and measure 3 1/2" diameter.

BADGE ORDER FORM

Date and details of walks completed..

....

NAME ....

ADDRESS ....

....

Price: £2.75 each including postage, VAT and signed completion certificate.
Amount enclosed (Payable to Trail Crest Publications) ..
From: **TRAIL CREST PUBLICATIONS Ltd.,** Milne House,
Speedwell Mill, Millers Green, Wirksworth, Derbyshire. DE4 4BL
© **/Fax** (0629) 826354 - 24hr answering service.

*********** YOU MAY PHOTOCOPY THIS FORM *********
"I'VE DONE A JOHN MERRILL WALK" T SHIRT -
Emerald Green with white lettering and walking man logo. Send £7.50 to Trail Crest Publications stating size required.
John Merrill's "Happy Walking!" Cap - £2.50

THE HIKER'S CODE

✿ *Hike only along marked routes - do not leave the trail.*

✿ *Use stiles to climb fences; close gates.*

✿ *Camp only in designated campsites.*

✿ *Carry a light-weight stove.*

✿ *Leave the trail cleaner than you found it.*

✿ *Leave flowers and plants for others to enjoy.*

✿ *Keep dogs on a leash.*

✿ *Protect and do not disturb wildlife.*

✿ *Use the trail at your own risk.*

✿ *Leave only your thanks and footprints - take nothing but photographs.*

NEW
BUTTON BADGES

- 58m.m. diameter
all at 30p each
- postage & packing 1 to 5 - 30p.

6 to 12 60p. 20 or more £1.00

	Quantity
JOHN MERRILL HAPPY WALKING BADGE	
FOOTSLOGGER BADGE	
WORLD'S SPEEDIEST HIKER	
WORLD'S DRIEST BOGTROTTER	
WORLD'S MOST CONFIDENT CLIMBER	
WORLD'S SLIMMEST BACKPACKER	
WORLD'S LEADING FELL RUNNER	
WORLD'S TIDIEST CAMPER	
WORLD'S LIGHTEST BACKPACKER	
WORLD'S HIGHEST OVERNIGHT CAMP	

Name..

Address ....

....

Amount enclosed payable to Trail Crest Publications Ltd. ....

"from footprint to finished book"

OTHER BOOKS by John N. Merrill Published by TRAIL CREST PUBLICATIONS Ltd.

YORKSHIRE DALES CHALLENGE WALK
NORTH YORKSHIRE MOORS CHALLENGE WALK
LAKELAND CHALLENGE WALK
THE RUTLAND WATER CHALLENGE WALK
MALVERN HILLS CHALLENGE WALK
THE SALTER'S WAY
THE SNOWDON CHALLENGE
CHARNWOOD FOREST CHALLENGE WALK
THREE COUNTIES CHALLENGE WALK (Peak District).

<u>INSTRUCTION & RECORD -</u>
HIKE TO BE FIT.....STROLLING WITH JOHN
THE JOHN MERRILL WALK RECORD BOOK

<u>MULTIPLE DAY WALKS -</u>
THE RIVERS'S WAY
PEAK DISTRICT: HIGH LEVEL ROUTE
PEAK DISTRICT MARATHONS
THE LIMEY WAY
THE PEAKLAND WAY

<u>COAST WALKS & NATIONAL TRAILS -</u>
ISLE OF WIGHT COAST PATH
PEMBROKESHIRE COAST PATH
THE CLEVELAND WAY
WALKING ANGELSEY'S COASTLINE.

<u>PEAK DISTRICT HISTORICAL GUIDES -</u>
A to Z GUIDE OF THE PEAK DISTRICT
DERBYSHIRE INNS - an A to Z guide
HALLS AND CASTLES OF THE PEAK DISTRICT & DERBYSHIRE
TOURING THE PEAK DISTRICT & DERBYSHIRE BY CAR
DERBYSHIRE FOLKLORE
PUNISHMENT IN DERBYSHIRE
CUSTOMS OF THE PEAK DISTRICT & DERBYSHIRE
WINTER - a souvenir guide
ARKWRIGHT OF CROMFORD
LEGENDS OF DERBYSHIRE
DERBYSHIRE FACTS & RECORDS
TALES FROM THE MINES by Geoffrey Carr
PEAK DISTRICT PLACE NAMES by Martin Spray

for a free copy
of the
**John Merrill
Walk Guide**
Catalogue
write to -
Trail Crest Publications Ltd.,

<u>JOHN MERRILL'S MAJOR WALKS -</u>
TURN RIGHT AT LAND'S END
WITH MUSTARD ON MY BACK
TURN RIGHT AT DEATH VALLEY
EMERALD COAST WALK

<u>SKETCH BOOKS -</u>
SKETCHES OF THE PEAK DISTRICT
<u>COLOUR BOOK:-</u>
THE PEAK DISTRICT......something to remember her by.

<u>OVERSEAS GUIDES -</u>
HIKING IN NEW MEXICO - Vol I - The Sandia and Manzano Mountains.
Vol 2 - Hiking "Billy the Kid" Country.
"WALKING IN DRACULA COUNTRY" - Romania.